B R I T A N N I A

The Royal Yacht Revealed

Lyndsey Bowditch

Blackboard Publishing Ltd

© BLACKBOARD PUBLISHING LTD 1998

Published by Blackboard Publishing Ltd
99 Giles Street, Edinburgh EH6 6BZ

Reprographics and Printing by Howie & Seath Ltd, Edinburgh

Binding by Hunter & Foulis Ltd, Edinburgh

Paper supplied by MoDo Merchants

A CIP catalogue record for this book is available from the British Library

ISBN 0 9534881 0 1

Throughout almost half a century of service the Royal Yacht *Britannia* generated excitement and admiration wherever she went in the world. The role played by the Yacht as an ambassador for Britain was unrivalled. Now, no longer in service, *Britannia* remains an important cultural icon of the 20th century.

It is fitting that at the end of her active life, *Britannia* should return to Scotland and to a familiar port for her final berth. Now permanently moored in Edinburgh's port of Leith, with its unique maritime and royal history going back many centuries, the Yacht's place in the nation's heritage is safeguarded for future generations.

Younger of Leckie

The Right Honourable Viscount Younger of Leckie KT KCVO TD DL
Chairman of The Former Royal Yacht Britannia Trust

Britannia is special for a number of reasons. Almost every previous sovereign has been responsible for building a church, a castle, a palace or just a house. The only comparable structure in the present reign is Britannia. As such she is a splendid example of contemporary British design and technology.

HRH Prince Philip

Charles II owned the first, but Charles III is unlikely ever to have one. For when the Royal Yacht *Britannia* was decommissioned on 11th December 1997, she became the last in a long line of Royal Yachts stretching back to 1660.

Plans to build a new Royal Yacht to replace the ageing *Victoria and Albert III* began in the reign of King George VI. But the King died in February 1952, four months before the keel of the Yacht was laid down. His daughter, Princess Elizabeth, inherited the ship along with the crown. On April 16th 1953, *Britannia* rolled down the slipway at John Brown's Clydebank Shipyard, and ever since then the Royal Yacht has held a special place in the Queen's heart. This was the ship which the Queen regarded as the one place where she could truly relax. Designed entirely to her wishes, *Britannia* is more closely associated with the Queen than any of her palaces or castles. Unlike her other royal residences, *Britannia* displays the Queen's taste uncluttered by the inheritance of previous generations.

The Royal Yacht was both promoter and protector of the Royal Family, providing not only the stage for the splendour of state occasions, but an impenetrable shield for the monarchy. A floating paradox, *Britannia* was the great public symbol of the monarchy and at the same time an utterly personal and private place to which the Royal Family could retire. She represents a complexity of contradictions. One of the most famous ships of the 20th century, but, until now, the least known. A ship on which it took three hours to set the table for a banquet, when the position of each knife, fork and spoon was meticulously measured with a ruler, but where the Princess of Wales could walk around barefoot, bikini-clad and licking a choc ice.

This was a ship which steamed over a million miles in the course of royal duty, a ship where Kings and Queens, Presidents and Prime Ministers were entertained, but a ship which, above all, was home to the world's most famous family.

Not a single rivet marks Britannia's streamlined hull. The ship's builders used internal butt straps to give a flush finish. The Queen approved the elegant gold line around the ship's hull, applied in thirty-four carat gold leaf.

The Building of Britannia

On 16th April 1953, Ship Number 691 waited at the top of the slipway in John Brown's Clydebank Shipyard. At 2.30pm precisely, a bottle of Empire wine hit her bow and the Queen pronounced that the 83rd Royal Yacht would be called *Britannia*. The name, which had been a closely guarded secret, drew gasps of surprise and delight from the waiting crowd, and as the band struck up a rendition of 'Rule Britannia' the crowd joined in with spontaneous song. And so the Royal Yacht *Britannia* was launched on the start of what would prove to be a long and illustrious career.

It was in 1938, some fifteen years previously, that the idea for a new Royal Yacht to replace the *Victoria and Albert III* was first considered. As well as serving as an official royal residence, the new Yacht was to double as a hospital ship in wartime, complete with dental surgery, laboratory, operating theatre and X-ray room. But the outbreak of World War II put plans on hold, and it was not until 1951 that the idea was revived. By then, King George VI's health was failing rapidly and the Government felt that a Royal Yacht could play some role in aiding his recovery. So a contract was placed with John Brown's Shipyard on the Clyde and work began in earnest. But it was to be in vain, for the King died four months before the keel of the Yacht was laid down.

The twenty-six year old Princess Elizabeth inherited the ship along with the crown. The new Queen together with her husband, Prince Philip, took a guiding hand in the design of the Yacht, approving plans and personally selecting furniture, fabrics and paintings. In a time of post-war austerity, economy was the watchword, and many items including furniture and even bed linen were brought from the *Victoria and Albert III* to be re-used on *Britannia*. The original budget set for the Yacht in 1938 was £900,000 but when work was finished in 1953 the total came to just over £2 million.

Although the ship was launched in 1953, there was still work to be completed on board and sea trials to be undertaken. It was not until January 1954 that the Royal Yacht was commissioned for service. In March of that year, *Britannia* sailed to Portsmouth where the First Sea Lord and the Controller inspected the Yacht. Security men swarmed on board to check for possible problems and an endless stream of requests to look round the Yacht were all politely but firmly refused. Much to its consternation, the press was not allowed on board and although the going rate for a photograph of the Queen's bedroom was £500, the price of a saloon car in 1954, no newspaper obtained the coveted picture.

Early in 1954, *Britannia's* Officers learnt that the Royal Yacht was to take Prince Charles and Princess Anne, then aged five and three, out to Tobruk to join their parents. On April 14th 1954 the Queen Mother and Princess Margaret handed over the children to the safekeeping of their governess, nurses and detective and *Britannia* set sail on her first of her 948 official voyages.

A Yacht is a necessity and not a luxury for the Head of our great British Commonwealth, between whose countries the sea is no barrier but the natural and indestructible highway.

HM The Queen

The late King George VI stressed this need for economy and made many suggestions with the object of reducing expenditure. The project was undertaken as a matter of urgency since it was the hope that a Yacht in which His Majesty could undertake sea voyages would greatly improve the chances of his recovery to good health.

Sir Victor Shephard, Director of Naval Construction

Laying the keel on June 16th 1952

The launching ceremony

The new Royal Yacht glides down the slipway

The ship in the fitting out basin

I name this ship Britannia. I wish success to her and all who sail in her.

HM The Queen

Britannia at the start of her illustrious career

You had to be on your toes when Prince Philip was on board. He was very keen and peppered us all with questions. There was one incident when he came on board when the winding gear for the Queen's embarkation ladder jammed. He promptly ordered it out. That was typical of him.

Dr John Brown, Naval Architect

The elegant sweeping staircase in the royal apartments

Britannia Revealed

The royal couple took a close interest in every aspect of the design. The Queen is a meticulous observer with very definite views on everything from the door-handles to the shape of the lampshades.

Sir Hugh Casson, Architect

The Royal Yacht *Britannia* presented a unique opportunity for the Queen and Prince Philip: the chance to design and furnish their new floating home entirely to their own taste. One of the first audiences which the new Queen gave was to the Controller of Navy Construction to discuss the proposals for *Britannia*, and she requested to meet with the architect responsible for the decorative scheme of the royal apartments. This was Mr J Patrick McBride of the Glasgow firm of architects, McInnes Gardner and Partners. McBride had previously worked for the Queen decorating the royal apartments on the Steamship *Gothic* for the Queen's Commonwealth Tour in 1953.

In July 1952 he had the first of many audiences with the Queen and Prince Philip to discuss their requirements for *Britannia*. By the following March, McBride had submitted the completed proposals for the royal apartments but the Queen and Prince Philip decided to seek a second opinion and consulted the Royal Society of Arts and the Council of Industrial Design. The outcome was that McBride's interiors were deemed too fussy, and in his place the architect, Sir Hugh Casson, was appointed.

Casson's interiors are simple and stylish and earned the praise of the Architect's Journal in 1954, which commented: 'The architect's restraint has retained an atmosphere of space which could have been easily destroyed.' Casson's approach, in its clean contemporary style and almost minimalist nature, epitomised modern post-war Britain. Throughout the royal apartments the white walls, brass metalwork and mahogany woodwork combine to produce light, airy and unpretentious interiors. To these, the Queen added the cool colours and chintzy furnishings reminiscent of the country house comfort which she so desired. The final cost for decorating and furnishing the royal apartments came to £78,000, an increase against the original budget of £60,000. Even then, many savings had been made by combining furniture from the earlier *Victoria and Albert* with specially bought new pieces.

Britannia *was rather special as far as we were concerned because we were involved from the very beginning in organising the design and furnishing and equipping and hanging of pictures, and for us it was rather special because all the other places we live in had been built by predecessors.*

HRH Prince Philip

The Royal Apartments

The Walmar baby grand piano cost £350 when it was supplied

The Waterford crystal glasses presented by John Brown's Shipyard

The portrait of Nelson which hangs on the Anteroom wall

The Drawing Room & Anteroom

The elegant Drawing Room is the main reception room in the royal apartments and was also the place where the Royal Family could relax, enjoying conversation, a game of cards or a musical recitation. The Drawing Room is divided from the Anteroom by polished mahogany folding doors which can be fully opened to make one eighteen-metre-long room. For official functions, the Drawing Room together with the Anteroom and Dining Room could accommodate up to 250 guests.

The Royal Family and their guests would gather in the Anteroom before lunch and dinner, and drinks would be served from the small pantry bar in the corner. As in most of the public rooms, the furnishings are a combination of antique and modern. The fine mahogany bookcase and the sideboard came from the King's study in the Royal Yacht *Victoria and Albert III*. In addition to the James Bond novels, royal favourites, the bookcase houses six Waterford crystal glasses and a tray presented to the Queen by John Brown's Shipyard to commemorate *Britannia's* launch. The more modern furniture in the Anteroom is Swedish and was given to the Queen by the Swedish royal family during the state visit to Stockholm in 1956.

The silver-grey carpet which stretches throughout the public rooms of the royal apartments was overlaid in the Drawing Room in 1979 with luxurious Persian rugs, gifted during the Queen's visit to the Arabian Gulf. The Drawing Room is tastefully furnished with chintz-covered sofas and armchairs which add to the feeling of country house comfort. Royal requests are not generally refused, but when the designs for this room were drawn up, the Queen's suggestion of an open coal fire was ultimately rejected.

Navy practice demanded that where there was an open fire, a sailor had to be on standby with a fire bucket at all times. As this might have spoiled the fireside ambience, an electric fire was chosen instead.

The Walmar baby grand piano in the corner of the Drawing Room cost £350 when it was supplied in 1953. It is firmly bolted to the deck to keep it secure in choppy seas. One of the most celebrated performers ever to sit at this piano was the playwright and composer Sir Noel Coward. He was invited by Princess Margaret to dine on board *Britannia* during a Caribbean cruise, and ended by singing for his supper. Amongst the Royal Family, Princess Diana, Princess Margaret and Princess Alexandra all enjoyed playing the baby grand in the Drawing Room. For more formal receptions, the resident pianist with the Royal Marines Band would sometimes provide background music as the Royal Family and their guests continued their after-dinner conversation.

There were always beautiful arrangements of flowers throughout the royal apartments and particularly in the Drawing Room. For state visits, flowers were always provided by the host country, but for UK voyages, hundreds of flowers would be picked from the gardens of Windsor Castle and stored in a special cold room below decks where they would keep fresh for several weeks. It was the job of *Britannia's* Stewards to acquaint themselves with the royal taste in flower arrangements and to provide the floral decorations when the Queen was aboard.

The elegant Drawing Room with its chintz furnishings and electric fire

The Anteroom where the Royal Family gathered for drinks before lunch and dinner

Elaborate interiors do look ridiculous at sea. Simplicity was the keynote - hence for example the grey carpeting which runs throughout the state apartments. I also wanted to show off the quality of light at sea. The overall idea was to give the impression of a country house at sea. I think we succeeded. Even today the Yacht looks very striking. She has an attractively old-fashioned air about her.

Sir Hugh Casson, Architect

The Dining Room table took three hours to set for a state banquet

Arabian kris with a horn and gold handle and gold chased scabbard

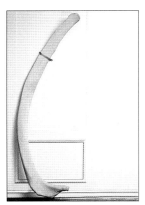

The whale rib bone collected by Prince Philip on Deception Island

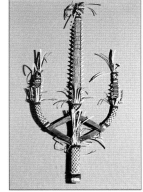

A sharks' teeth ceremonial trident from the Solomon Islands

The position of each knife, fork and spoon was meticulously measured with a ruler

The Dining Room

Throughout the forty-four years of *Britannia's* life, the royal Dining Room has witnessed some spectacular banquets and played host to the rich, the famous and the powerful. Sir Winston Churchill, Rajiv Ghandi, Nelson Mandela, Bill Clinton, Boris Yeltsin, Ronald Reagan and Margaret Thatcher have all accepted the ultimate honour to dine at the table of Her Majesty The Queen aboard the Royal Yacht.

It took three hours to set the fifty-six places for a state banquet, and the position of every knife, fork and spoon was meticulously measured with a ruler. Grace was never said and ashtrays only brought to the table at the end of the meal. The menus, which were printed in French before *Britannia* set sail, were given to each guest to keep as a souvenir of a very special night.

Even when there was no official entertaining on board *Britannia*, the same standards and formality prevailed and the Royal Family would dress for dinner accompanied by the Admiral and senior members of the royal household. When Princess Margaret and her new bridegroom, Anthony Armstrong-Jones, spent their honeymoon on *Britannia* in 1960, the Princess donned a formal evening dress and tiara each evening for dinner.

As well as the venue for spectacular state receptions, the Dining Room has served as a cinema, a dance hall and a church. For film shows, the large white panels at the end of the room hinged back to reveal the housing for twin film projectors. While the younger members of the Royal Family preferred the latest Walt Disney creation, the more mature members favoured comedies and James Bond movies. The carpet could be rolled up to expose a wooden dance floor beneath; the last time

this was used was for Princess Anne's twenty-first birthday celebrations in 1971.

On Sundays, the Dining Room took on a more solemn air when it was used for church services. Unusually, for a ship of her size, *Britannia* did not have her own chaplain. This was the Queen's decision in 1953 and proved controversial at the time. The fifteen-minute Sunday service, comprising three hymns accompanied by the Royal Marines Band, a short address and a Bible reading, was taken instead by *Britannia's* Admiral and was the only occasion when all ranks were given permission to enter the royal apartments.

The Dining Room is also home to many of the exotic gifts which were given to the Queen and Prince Philip on their voyages in *Britannia*. Among these number the long string of red feather money from Santa Cruz presented to Prince Philip in 1957 and reportedly worth £15 at the time, a two-metre-long whale rib bone picked up from a beach on Deception Island by Prince Philip in the same year, and a conch shell collected in the Caribbean in 1966. More ornate are the ivory, gold and silver swords and daggers presented during visits to Malaysia in 1972 and Arabia in 1979. Other reminders of trips to far-flung places include sharks' teeth swords from the Solomon Islands, arrows and boomerangs

from Australia, a fan made from the head and tail feathers of a New Guinean bird of paradise, and a bone and mother-of-pearl necklace given to the Queen in Tuvalu in the Pacific Islands.

Some of the more unusual presents not to be found in the Dining Room included a giant tortoise presented in the Seychelles, a baby crocodile given to the Queen in a pierced silver biscuit tin during a visit to the Gambia, which later ended up in the bath of the Queen's Private Secretary, and an enormous roast pig brought on board by the natives of Fiji.

During the royal visit to the Arabian Gulf in 1979, the Queen was given over one million pounds' worth of presents, including diamond studded watches, huge natural pearls, a gold handbag, a pinafore of gold chainmail and the Persian rugs which were placed in the Drawing Room. The Queen's gifts in return tend to be more modest. At the start of each state visit, gifts were brought on board to be presented during the trip. They rarely varied: cuff links and wallets for men, brooches and powder boxes for women, and for the chosen few, framed signed photographs of the Queen herself. In 1991 the royal purse spent £34,000 on gifts to be dispensed during *Britannia's* official visits.

The crystal glasses are all engraved with the Queen's cypher

EⅡR

MENU

Gleneagles Pate

———

Suprême of Chicken with Wild Mushrooms
Salad

———

Chocolate and Ginger Mousse

WINES
Sancerre 1995
Château Arnauld 1990
Harveys Vintage Port 1983

Tuesday 13th May 1997   Bangkok

The menu which was served during a state banquet in Bangkok in 1997

The Queen's Sitting Room

Located between the Dining Room and the Drawing Room on the Upper Deck are the private Sitting Rooms, or day cabins, of the Queen and Prince Philip. The Queen's room is on the starboard side and Prince Philip's, which is a mirror image, is on the port side. Both the Queen and Prince Philip used these rooms principally as offices where they worked on state business. Even at sea the business of the monarchy never stopped. The red boxes containing state papers would be flown or shipped out to *Britannia* daily no matter where she was in the world. Each day the Queen would spend several hours working in her Sitting Room on these papers and holding audiences with her Private and Press Secretaries.

The two-metre-long built-in desk with its green leather top was where the Queen sat to work and here the royal writing paper, pens and blotters were kept. The green upholstered sofa complements the moss green carpet and was originally used in HMS *Vanguard* in 1947, when King George VI, his wife and his daughter, Princess Elizabeth, travelled to South Africa. The gold-leaf light brackets in the design of wheatsheaves came from the Steamship *Gothic*. At one end of the room, above the electric fire is an intricate gilt mirror in the style of a ship's wheel topped with a gold crown, which cost £315 in 1953. At the opposite end of the room is the built-in bookcase where the Queen kept many of her personal books.

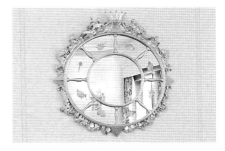

The gilt mirror is carved with figures of Neptune and a mermaid

The wall lights are designed in the shape of wheatsheaves

Hugh Casson was the expert concerned with the interior decorating of the royal apartments and we saw a lot of him. I remember his insistence that a beautiful circular mirror in Her Majesty's Sitting Room should be at such a height that its centre was at the precise height of her eyes.

Captain J S Dalglish

The Queen's Sitting Room was used mainly as an office by Her Majesty to attend to state business

The Duke's Sitting Room

While the Queen's Sitting Room was reserved for her use alone, Prince Philip's study was used by both himself and Prince Charles. The teak-panelled walls and red leather topped desk lend a functional look to the room. Above the desk is a specially designed display case which holds a model of HMS *Magpie*, the Duke's first naval command. Like the Queen, Prince Philip also had a built-in bookcase in his Sitting Room where he kept favourite books.

Both the Queen's and Prince Philip's Sitting Rooms are connected by telephone to each other and to the offices of their Private Secretaries, one deck below. The telephone system in the Royal Yacht is identical to that used at Buckingham Palace. For top-secret messages, conversations on the royal telephones can be 'scrambled' to ensure ultimate security.

The Duke's Sitting Room has a functional look

The model of HMS Magpie takes pride of place above the Duke's desk

The royal telephones are identical to those in Buckingham Palace

The Royal Bedrooms

One level above the Main Deck is the Shelter Deck where the four principal royal bedrooms are situated. Both the Queen's and Prince Philip's bedroom suites are on the starboard side, and each has its own bathroom complete with 1950s chrome fittings and thermometer to ensure the correct bath temperature. A connecting door links the two bedrooms, both of which are furnished with a single bed. The windows here are purposely higher than elsewhere on the Yacht to prevent accidental glimpses into the bedrooms from the deck outside.

The public viewing of the Queen's bedroom on *Britannia* marks a first, for never before has the bedroom of a living monarch been seen. Like the rest of the royal apartments, the bedrooms lack ostentation and are remarkable for their display of relatively modest royal taste. The Queen eschewed the fashion for duvets in favour of floral bedspreads. The embroidered silk panel above the bed adds a touch of country house elegance and femininity. It was especially commissioned in 1953 at a cost of £450. The Queen's frugal streak shows through in her decision to use the bed linen originally bought for Queen Victoria's bedroom on the previous Royal Yacht. However, the Queen's sheets were specially tailored to Her Majesty's preference, with a deep turnback and embossed with the personal monogram, 'HM The Queen'.

The embroidered panel above the Queen's bed adds a touch of country house elegance

The Queen's bedroom remains intact with its original 1950s furniture

The small built-in desk in the Queen's bedroom

The Duke of Edinburgh's bedroom has a similar layout to Her Majesty's, but reflecting the Duke's personal taste has a more masculine look. Like the Queen, Prince Philip preferred to have blankets rather than a duvet on his bed, but as he did not require the same deep turnback, the Duke's sheets are slightly smaller. His pillowcases are the same size as the Queen's, but on his specific request do not have the lace borders. Each of the royal beds has a panel equipped with a buzzer, and one simple press of this at any time of day or night, would summon a Steward to bring food or drink.

On the same deck level are the wardrobe rooms where the Queen's clothes, jewels and accessories were kept, under the watchful eye of Her Majesty's dresser. On formal visits, the Queen would sometimes change clothes up to five times a day, and her dressers were responsible for ensuring that the Queen's immaculate outfits and accessories were always ready. Prince Philip had his own valet to attend to his wardrobe whose job it was to ensure that the Duke always appeared wearing the correct medals or decorations on each state occasion.

Two further royal bedrooms which adjoin are situated on the port side of the Shelter Deck. While the Queen's and Prince Philip's rooms were reserved for their sole use, the bedrooms on the port side were used by other members of the Royal Family. One of these rooms contains *Britannia's* only double bed and formed the honeymoon suite for the four pairs of newlyweds who honeymooned on the Yacht. When the royal children were small, these two bedrooms were sometimes used as nursery suites.

In addition to the four bedrooms on this level, there are a further sixteen cabins on the deck below, twelve of which had en-suite bathrooms. These rooms were used by members of the Royal Family and their guests, as well as by the royal household. Cabin Fourteen which had gold-coloured furnishings was

reputedly favoured by both Prince Charles and Prince Edward. This level also has the only suite of rooms in the whole of the royal apartments, consisting of two cabins with en-suite bathrooms and a central sitting room. It was usually given to the most senior guests, and it was here that President and Mrs Clinton stayed during their visit in 1994. The same suite was used by Mr and Mrs Patten, on their return from the handover of Hong Kong in 1997.

A connecting door links Prince Philip's bedroom to the Queen's room

The dark timber furniture lends a more masculine feel to Prince Philip's bedroom

Britannia's only bedroom containing a double bed formed the honeymoon suite on board

Outside the royal bedrooms the walls of the vestibule are lined with family photographs

The elaborate light fitting in the vestibule

The Vestibule & Verandah Deck

The vestibule outside the royal bedrooms leads to the Sun Lounge and the Verandah, the largest deck on *Britannia*. This was a secluded part of the ship where the Royal Family could relax in privacy, sunbathing or enjoying games of quoits or deck hockey. Prince Philip would occasionally set up his easel and indulge in the royal pastime of painting. There was even a collapsible swimming pool which was sometimes placed here for the royal children to take a dip in. The Verandah Deck was also used during formal state occasions for receptions and sometimes for group photographs. Then the Queen and her guests of honour would line up, and the ship's photographer, 'Snaps', would set up his camera to record another historic moment.

The Sun Lounge

The beautiful timber-lined Sun Lounge was one of the Queen's favourite spaces in *Britannia*. The Queen would take breakfast and afternoon tea in this room while enjoying the often spectacular views through the large picture windows. The formica wall panels, with illustrations of former royal yachts, conceal a refrigerated drinks cabinet on one side and a record and games store on the other. The bamboo furniture was bought by Prince Philip in 1959 during his visit to Hong Kong.

A 1950s wicker chair echoes the shape of the porthole

The blue patterned sofa sits opposite the picture windows

The rum tub was used until 1970 to issue the Yachtsmen's daily rum ration

The base of the mizzen mast cuts through the beautiful timber-lined Sun Lounge, one of the Queen's favourite rooms in Britannia

Britannia really combines two ships in one: part royal, part Navy. The main mast marks the mid point of the Yacht and divides it in two. Forward of the mast is the working part of the ship where the 260 Officers and Yachtsmen lived and worked. The rather cramped conditions in this part of the ship were typical of any 1950s warship, and were in marked contrast to the luxury and comfort of the royal apartments, which occupied an area roughly equal in size. The royal quarters, situated aft of the main mast, provided accommodation for the Royal Family and the forty-five members of their household who travelled with the Queen on official visits.

1. Ensign Mast
2. Mizzen Mast
3. Main Mast
4. Fore Mast
5. Jackstaff
6. Quarter Deck
7. The Drawing Room
8. The Anteroom
9. Verandah Deck
10. The Sun Lounge
11. Royal Bedrooms
12. The Queen's Bathroom
13. The Queen's Bedroom
14. The Duke's Bedroom
15. The Duke's Bathroom
16. Maid's Room
17. Pantry
18. Wardrobe Room
19. Valets' Bedrooms
20. The Queen's Sitting Room
21. The Dining Room
22. Servery

23.	Staff Cabins	34.	Clerks' Office	45.	Activity Boat	56.	Sick Bay & Operating Theatre	67.	Stokers' Mess
24.	Royal Household Cabins	35.	Main Turbine Engine Room	46.	Jolly Boat	57.	Boiler Rooms	68.	Cold Rooms
25.	Master of the Household's Cabin	36.	Baggage Rooms	47.	Compass Platform	58.	Bathrooms	69.	Platform Deck
26.	The Equerry's Sitting Room	37.	Linen Stores	48.	Officers' Cabins	59.	Showers	70.	Store
27.	Cloak Room	38.	Blanket Stores	49.	Radar Scanner	60.	Auxiliary Room	71.	Main Deck Mess
28.	Lower Entrance	39.	Wine Stores	50.	Royal Bridge	61.	Laundry	72.	Lower Deck Store Rooms
29.	Guest Suite	40.	China Stores	51.	Shelter Deck	62.	Yachtsmen's Mess	73.	Shipwrights' Workshop
30.	Cabin	41.	Fuel Tanks	52.	Upper Deck	63.	Stabiliser Compartment		
31.	Maid's Sitting Room	42.	Dinghies	53.	Anchor Cables & Capstans	64.	Engineers' Workshop		
32.	Staff Cabins	43.	Motor Boat	54.	Air Conditioning Plant	65.	Chief Petty Officers' Cabin		
33.	Royal Clerks' Office	44.	Royal Barge	55.	Ship's Doctor's Room	66.	Auxiliary Machine Room		

The Working Ship

The Flag Deck & Boat Deck

The Flag Deck is the highest part of the Royal Yacht, and it was from here that *Britannia's* flag and light signalling was conducted. Signal flags, used to send messages to passing ships, were hoisted from the halyards, the ropes on either side of the fore mast. Also on the Flag Deck are the twelve-inch and ten-inch signal lights which *Britannia* used to flash messages in Morse Code to ships nearby. In the 1970s modern satellite communications were introduced on board *Britannia*. The large white dome

on the Flag Deck is the aerial for this system, and is one of the few additions to alter *Britannia's* external appearance.

As a Ship of State, the Royal Yacht has three masts: the fore mast which is situated on the Flag Deck, the main mast which splits the ship in two and the mizzen mast, towards the stern of the ship. Hidden beneath the base of each of the masts are a number of coins which were placed there in 1953 as payment to the angels to guard the souls of the sailors at sea. And there they remain to

this day. Each of the masts is topped with a gold finial which is actually a radio aerial.

Britannia's standards were high. Even the ship's funnel, which housed a tiny multi-gym for the Royal Yachtsmen, was specially designed with a gutter to stop raindrops splashing and staining the pale paintwork. Below the funnel is the Boat Deck. *Britannia* carried more craft than a warship and here the Yacht's ten boats and eighteen life rafts were stowed.

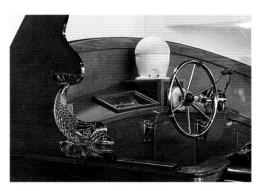

The wheel of the Royal Barge

A decorative dolphin on the Royal Barge

Britannia's *boats are stowed on overhead davits*

The flag locker where the signal flags are stored

The Bridge retains its original 1950s appearance

Britannia *was steered from the Wheelhouse, below decks*

The Bridge

Britannia's nerve centre was the Bridge. With its wooden binnacle and chrome voice pipes, through which orders were issued to the Wheelhouse, the Bridge still retains its original 1950s appearance. The radar and other navigational equipment were the only modern introductions to the Bridge. Somewhat cramped by today's standards, the Bridge was *Britannia's* command point and one of the most important places on the Yacht. It was from here that the Officers navigated, here log books were recorded, orders issued, and every mile of the ship's progress planned and plotted.

In addition to the Officer of the Watch, who was in overall charge, there would normally be a Lookout and a Signalman stationed on the Bridge when *Britannia* was at sea. Together it was their job to ensure that everything went according to plan. But the man with the ultimate responsibility for *Britannia* and the safety of the Queen and crew was the Admiral, *Britannia's* Captain. The only chair in the room was for his use alone. In this high-pressured environment, everyone else was expected to be upstanding, always on the alert, for this was no place to relax.

A metal voice pipe through which orders were issued

The Wheelhouse

Britannia's Wheelhouse was situated on the deck immediately below the Bridge. Although it seems unusual to steer a ship from below decks, it was traditionally thought to provide some protection in case of attack on the more vulnerable Bridge. The two pipes in the ceiling of the Wheelhouse were linked to the Bridge, and the Officers would speak into them to instruct the men in the Wheelhouse below on the direction to steer the ship. There would normally be three men in the Wheelhouse: one to steer the ship, and two to operate the brass engine telegraphs on either side of the wheel. These telegraphs were linked by mechanical rod gearing to the Engine Room five decks below and were used to pass orders on the ship's speed and movement.

The ship's wheel came from the racing yacht *Britannia* which was originally built in 1893 for the Prince of Wales, who later became King Edward VII. The Yacht then passed to King George V, the Queen's grandfather, and although she was scuttled in 1936 the wheel was rescued and later installed in the Royal Yacht *Britannia*.

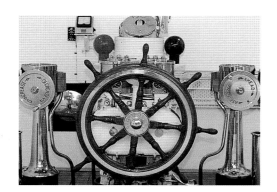

Britannia's *wheel which came from King Edward VII's yacht*

The Engine Room

The gleaming Engine Room of the Royal Yacht *Britannia* is a proud testament to 1950s British marine engineering. It has barely changed throughout the forty-four years of *Britannia's* life and practically every piece of machinery, every gadget, stopcock, switch and dial has operated faultlessly since *Britannia* first set sail in 1953.

When America's General Norman Schwarzkopf was shown *Britannia's* spotless Engine Room in 1992, he was reported as saying: 'Okay. I've seen the museum piece. Now, where's the real Engine Room?' And with its chrome dials and old fashioned steam turbines, the Engine Room does have an air of antiquity.

The two pairs of high and low pressure steam turbine engines, which have never been completely opened, carried *Britannia* over one million miles, the equivalent of once round the globe for every year of her life. The engines are capable of developing a total of 12,000 horse power, and drive the Yacht at twenty-one knots: a speed that *Britannia* was capable of providing throughout her life.

Britannia's immaculate Engine Room is a proud testament to British marine engineering

One of the ship's steam turbine engines, which has never been completely opened

The Generator & Boiler Rooms

Located next to the Engine Room is the Boiler Room with its maze of pipes and wires. It contains two Foster Wheeler 'D' type boilers which until 1983 burned furnace fuel before being converted to diesel. Steam passed from the boilers into the Engine Room turbines through the large white pipes. The turbines then connected to the gear boxes which, in turn, were linked by thirty-metre-long shafts to the ship's two propellers.

At the front of the Engine Room, the sparkling chrome dials were used to monitor the different stages of steam pressures and vacuums. These were critical for ensuring the safe passage of *Britannia*. Manning the Engine and Boiler Rooms was labour intensive and amongst the Yacht's crew there numbered some eighty engineers. At any one time there would be eight men on duty in the Engine, Boiler and associated machinery rooms.

The Royal Yacht operated on a 225 volt direct current run by steam generators. The Yacht also had one back-up diesel generator which was affectionately known as 'Chitty-Chitty Bang-Bang'. This engine originally came from HM Submarine *Vampire* and was put into *Britannia* as the auxiliary diesel engine in 1953. In 1997, just before the Yacht was decommissioned, it was reported to be oldest working diesel in the world.

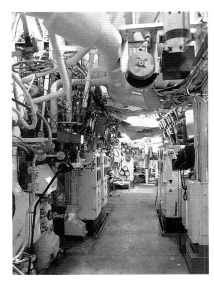

The Boiler Room houses two Foster Wheeler 'D' type boilers

Any two of the Yacht's three turbo generators are capable of meeting the ship's electricity requirement

The Garage

When *Britannia* was built in 1953, a garage to house the Phantom V Rolls Royce, or occasionally the royal Land Rover, was considered an absolute essential. But getting the vehicle on board was less than straight-forward. First, the car, in its transporter, had to be hoisted onto the special trackway which is fitted into the deck. Even then, it could only be squeezed into the Garage by removing its bumpers. In more recent times this procedure proved too complicated and, as a suitable car could usually be found in the country that the Queen was visiting, the Rolls was rarely carried.

Hoisting the Rolls Royce on board was a complicated procedure

The Admiral's Suite

The living accommodation for *Britannia*'s Admiral and senior Officers is situated at the front of the Royal Yacht. Throughout her life *Britannia* was captained by nine Admirals and latterly a Commodore and each in turn occupied the Admiral's Suite. This comprised a day cabin, a sleeping cabin and a bathroom. Not only did the Admiral have ultimate responsibility for ensuring the smooth running of *Britannia*, but he was also in charge of a staff of some nineteen Officers and 240 Yachtsmen. As befits his standing, the Admiral's Suite is the most spacious and comfortable accommodation outside the royal apartments.

The day cabin was where the Admiral worked, entertained and often ate during his time on board. Here he would plan for the weeks and often months ahead which would be spent at sea. Sitting at his desk, he would write official letters and reports on the ship's progress. At the long mahogany table he would hold meetings with his senior Officers to plan strategies and delegate duties, and here he would interview each new recruit to *Britannia*, from the most junior Yachtsman to the highest ranking Officer.

The Admiral would use his room for more relaxing and sociable events too, perhaps a dinner or drinks party for specially invited guests. When the Queen, the Duke of Edinburgh or any of the Royal Family were on board, the Admiral would always dine with them in the royal Dining Room. But when there were no royal passengers, he would normally eat alone in his room, allowing his fellow Officers the chance to unwind away from the boss.

A connecting door leads from the Admiral's day cabin to his sleeping cabin with its single bed and row of sycamore-veneered wardrobes. These held his uniforms, and with up to twelve changes of clothes a day his uniforms always had to be immaculate. The sleeping cabin links to the bathroom with its original chrome fittings and which contains one of the few baths in this part of the ship.

The sofa and armchairs came from the Victoria and Albert III *and are over 100 years old*

The long mahogany table was where the Admiral conducted meetings and where he sat to eat

The Officers' Cabins & Ratings' Berths

If conditions for the nineteen Officers were cramped and austere, there was even less living space and practically no privacy for the 240 crew. The Officers' cabins have changed little since they were first used in 1954. The fold-down beds still lift up to make daytime seats, the bakelite handles on the cupboards and wardrobes have gained a patina with age and the stainless steel washbasins gleam with forty years of polishing. As well as serving as a sleeping berth, each Officer's cabin doubled as an office. In these relatively cramped conditions they were expected to do their report writing and to store all their files, uniforms and personal possessions. Despite their high status, none of the Officers enjoyed the luxury of an en-suite bathroom, and they had to make do instead with shared facilities.

The senior Officers' accommodation shares a landing and corridor with the Admiral's Suite. This area was quickly dubbed the 'Whispering Gallery' by the crew, although whether it was the Officers or the crew doing the whispering is not quite clear. On the deck below are the tiny cubby holes where the junior Officers lived in an area they named 'The Ghetto'. Although conditions for the Yachtsmen were improved during the 1973 refit when the hammocks throughout were exchanged for bunks, a Yachtsman could expect little luxury and no privacy. Toilet and washing facilities are typical of any 1950s' warship, but would not pass muster with today's Navy recruits.

Hierarchy was strongly defined on *Britannia* and was reflected in everything from the food to the sleeping arrangements. The Admiral, at the top of the tree, had his own comfortable quarters and generally ate alone in his room. Next in line were the Officers. Senior Officers had larger cabins than the junior Officers, but all were equally welcome in the Wardroom where they donned formal wear for dinner each evening. Next in the pecking order were the Warrant and Chief Petty Officers who shared sleeping quarters, but had their own Mess with elegant white panelling and mementoes from the Royal Yacht *Victoria and Albert III*. Like all the Royal Yachtsmen, they took their main meal in the middle of the day rather than in the evening. Below them came the Petty Officers and Sergeants whose cramped sleeping quarters were only somewhat compensated for by the welcoming atmosphere of their adjoining Mess with its bar nicknamed the 'Verge Inn'. At the bottom were the Leading and Able Seamen who lived in extremely confined conditions and shared a Mess known as the Unwinding Room. Its bar gained the dubious title of 'Ye old Honk Inn'. Separate from the Royal Yachtsmen was *Britannia's* contingent of Royal Marines who formed the band and carried out security duties. They had their own Mess, called The Barracks.

The Officers' beds fold up to make a seat for day-time use

The First Lieutenant's cabin, which is typical of the senior Officers' accommodation in Britannia

Living conditions for the Yachtsmen were cramped and austere

The Wardroom table set for dinner

The Wardroom

The Wardroom was where *Britannia's* nineteen Officers, loyal subjects whose duty was to serve the Queen, would gather daily for meals and to unwind after a long stint on duty. Strictly off limits to the rest of the crew, the Wardroom was a sort of gentlemen's club afloat where tradition was the watchword.

Breakfast and lunch were fairly informal and the Officers could come and go as they pleased, but dinner was an altogether different affair. In the evening the Officers sporting the 'Red Sea Rig', the traditional Naval uniform at sea of a white shirt, black trousers, patent leather shoes and cummerbund would gather in the Anteroom next to the Wardroom for pre-dinner drinks. A number of the junior Yachtsmen acted as Naval Stewards, and it was their job

to serve the fine cuisine prepared by the Wardroom Galley chefs and the excellent wines, brought up from *Britannia's* wine cellar. The Officers dined extremely well and for a special occasion a menu might comprise: Seafood Crepes, followed by Fillet of Beef Britannia served with Pommes Hongroise, cauliflower and courgettes, rounded off with Apricot Ice Cream Bombe and Champagne Sorbet. And for that touch of flair, the Royal Marines Band, when not on royal duty, would provide musical accompaniment to the meal.

On formal evenings, tradition dictated that the Officers took turns at composing a rhyming Grace. What they lacked in metre, they made up for in irreverence:

As we savour your bounteous gifts
Let us not forget - for it would be so remiss
Those whose table is not so fine
Who will not today share sparkling wine
For tonight O Lord, as we dine from plates, full
Be assured we are most grateful!
Amen

At the end of the meal the Officers stood to drink the loyal toast to Her Majesty The Queen, and the Royal Marines Band would play the National Anthem. Finally, to round off an altogether stylish evening, the 'Youngest Unheard Officer' would be invited to entertain his colleagues with an amusing after dinner speech.

The Anteroom

The Anteroom adjoins the Wardroom and, with the bar as its focus, it was the Officers' main recreational space. Here they would get together not only for drinks but to watch television, listen to the radio, play mess games or take part in *Britannia's* fiercely contested Yacht quizzes.

One memorable game peculiar to the Wardroom was 'Wombat Tennis'. This pitted the junior Officers against their seniors. The quarry was a soft toy wombat which had been donated by a Lady-in-Waiting on the understanding that it would receive love and affection. The game commenced in earnest when the wombat was thrown up into the ceiling fan and the batting began. Normally the game ended with one side mounting a pitch invasion on the other, but it was generally the wombat who came off worst. It was a regular patient in the Sick Bay where the Ship's Doctor would stitch it back together in preparation for the next round.

Another toy animal who made his home in the Anteroom was the small wooden monkey. He arrived on board during the Queen's visit to Copenhagen in 1957, and although no Officer was ever allowed to touch him, he mysteriously moved round the Wardroom to be found in a different hiding-place each day.

Although this was the venue for the Officers to unwind and indulge in a bit of light-hearted relief, these rooms would often take on a more formal atmosphere; at no time more so than when the Queen and the Duke of Edinburgh or other members of the Royal Family were entertained here for dinner or a drinks party. Then etiquette prevailed once more.

The Wardroom and the Anteroom also house a sumptuous collection of nineteenth-century silver, much of which came from previous royal yachts. The silver sailing ship is the top part of a huge salt cellar reputedly owned by the last Czar of Russia. The silver Pegasus bowl with its flying horse handles was presented to the Wardroom by the Officers of the *Victoria and Albert III* and depicts four earlier royal yachts. One of the most treasured items in the Wardroom Collection is the small gold button which came from Admiral Nelson's coat.

Nelson's button takes pride of place in the Anteroom

The Pegasus bowl depicts four former royal yachts

The wombat waits in his lair

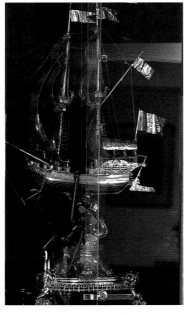

The silver salt reputedly owned by the Czar

The Anteroom was the one place where the Officers could unwind

The Queen and her Private Secretary, Sir Martin Charteris, work late into the night on a speech for the following day

Although it was well after midnight the Queen and her Private Secretary Sir Martin Charteris were still working on a speech the Queen was to give at the state opening of Parliament in Mauritius the next day. Not many people realise just what long hours are worked by the Queen and her staff.

Lord Lichfield

A Royal Residence

Britannia had a unique status, combining the formality of a floating palace with the holiday atmosphere of a cruise ship. This was the ship, which even with its staff of around 300, could lead the Queen to remark that it was the one place where she could truly relax.

Unlike the Queen's other royal residences, *Britannia's* modern interiors reveal the royal taste uncluttered by the inheritance of previous generations. The royal quarters are stylish and understated. Since *Britannia's* royal apartments are contained within a ship, they are smaller than those of the Queen's other official residences ashore, but there is a more significant difference.

Traditionally royal apartments, such as those in Buckingham Palace or Windsor Castle, are used only for formal occasions, but on *Britannia* the royal apartments were in daily use. It is this glimpse of the private, informal face of the monarchy, normally carefully concealed, which *Britannia* so tantalisingly reveals.

With reassuringly familiar rooms, full of family photographs and much-loved personal possessions, *Britannia* provided an unwavering welcome for the Queen no matter where she was in the world. It was to *Britannia* that the Queen came home.

Britannia *is to be at times the home of my husband and myself and of our family.*

HM The Queen

A Day In The Life

Depending on whether Her Majesty was on an official state visit or merely spending time on *Britannia* travelling from one destination to another, the Queen's day would vary greatly. Although no two days were ever the same, a day when the Queen was 'at home' on *Britannia* might have gone something like this . . .

7·30 AM
Her Majesty The Queen is woken by her personal maid and is served a cup of tea with milk. The maid prepares the Queen's bath to the correct temperature, which she checks with a thermometer.

8·30 AM
The Queen takes breakfast in the Sun Lounge.

9·15 AM
After breakfast, the Queen retires to her Sitting Room to start work with her Private Secretary on the 'boxes' of official documents which arrive daily on *Britannia* from various Government departments.

11·00 AM
Coffee break and a chance for the Queen to view the chart in the Sun Lounge showing *Britannia's* position and distance travelled overnight.

11·30 AM
Back to work on the official papers until lunchtime.

1·00 PM
The Queen and members of the Royal Family gather in the Dining Room for a buffet lunch.

2·30 PM
The Queen spends the afternoon working on private correspondence.

5·00 PM
Time for afternoon tea. This is taken in the Sun Lounge and would invariably consist of wafer-thin cucumber and smoked salmon sandwiches, pastries and gateaux, served with tea in the finest bone china cups.

6·00 PM
Her Majesty retires to meet with her dresser to discuss jewellery and dress requirements for the evening.

7·00 PM
The Queen dresses for dinner in her bedroom.

7·30 PM
The Royal Family gather in the Anteroom for drinks with the Admiral of the Yacht and senior members of the royal household before moving through to the royal Dining Room.

8·00 PM
Dinner is served, for family occasions on the white and gold china. The green and white Spode china decorated with the royal cypher is used for dessert.

9·30 PM
The Royal Family retire to the Drawing Room for coffee, liqueurs and chocolate mints. The rest of the evening may be spent playing cards, doing jigsaw puzzles or just enjoying conversation.

11·00 PM
The Queen retires to bed, and everybody follows suit.

At Home In Britannia

Prince Charles, aged five, takes
Britannia's helm in 1954

The Queen Mother meets some of the Yachtsmen
in their messdeck during a visit to Canada in 1967

Master Peter Phillips, and LSEA 'Wiggy' Bennett get
ready for the order to slip anchor in 1988

On the Royal Bridge, with President Eisenhower during
the opening of the St Lawrence Seaway in 1959

The Royal Family at ease on Britannia as the Royal Yacht sets sail for the last Western Isles cruise in July 1997

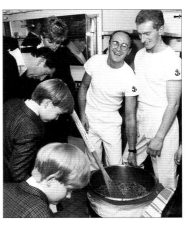

Princess Anne talks to her great-uncle, Earl
Mountbatten, on the Verandah Deck in 1969

Princess Beatrice celebrates her first birthday with her mother, the
Duchess of York, and some of Britannia's Yachtsmen in 1989

The Prince and Princess of Wales and their sons stir
the Christmas Pudding in Britannia's galley in 1991

Princess Diana throws royal protocol to the winds as she
rushes to greet her sons on Britannia in Toronto in 1991

Prince William and Peter Phillips greet each other during the
Royal Family's last voyage to the Western Isles in 1997

The Prince and Princess of Wales wave goodbye as they set sail from Gibraltar in 1981

The Duke and Duchess of York's honeymoon cruise took them to the Azores

Princess Anne takes a photograph while on honeymoon with Captain Mark Phillips in 1973

Princess Margaret and Anthony Armstrong-Jones bid farewell to Britannia's crew in 1960

Princess Diana prepares to embark on Britannia for her honeymoon

I was in the scullery washing up plates when I heard a voice in the servery. I went out to look to find a newly wed Princess sitting on the freezer in a bikini, flip flops and hat, licking a choc ice.

Leading Steward Mark Elliot

A Romantic Retreat

Royal honeymoons always attract international attention but *Britannia* was to prove the perfect antidote, providing privacy for the four couples who honeymooned on board. Out of range of the press photographers' lenses, a week or a fortnight spent on *Britannia* was as near to seclusion as the Royal Family ever got. But for Princess Margaret and Anthony Armstrong-Jones, the first royal honeymooners to enjoy *Britannia's* star treatment in 1960, it was not without controversy. The Labour MP, Emrys Hughes, raised the question of cost in the House of Commons. Although he was told that the wages of the Officers and crew would be paid regardless of whether *Britannia* sailed or not, the answer managed to overlook the cost of taking the yacht on a 6,000 mile voyage to the Caribbean. When the time came for the royal couple to set sail from London's River Thames, any ill-feeling had died away and they were cheered by vast crowds of well-wishers. Throughout the trip the crew went to great lengths to ensure the honeymoon was a success, ensuring the couple's privacy, organising

trips on shore and anticipating every royal wish. Princess Margaret later said: 'It was so very wonderful for us both, just to lie on those deserted beaches without a soul in sight.'

The next honeymooners, too, did not have an idyllic start. The first week of Princess Anne's and Captain Mark Phillips' honeymoon in the West Indies in 1973 was blighted by violent storms. Captain Phillips later reported, 'For the first four days we were both seasick.' But the twenty-foot waves eventually subsided and the thunder clouds cleared allowing the honeymoon to continue in more favourable circumstances.

In 1981, the Prince and Princess of Wales flew to Gibraltar to meet *Britannia* at the start of their sixteen-day honeymoon voyage to the Mediterranean. The twenty-year old Princess quickly introduced her informal style to the Yacht and during the honeymoon the royal couple rarely used the formal state apartments, preferring the relaxed atmosphere of the Sun Lounge and the Verandah Deck. Princess Diana enjoyed exploring *Britannia's* lower decks and

was frequently to be seen peering into cupboards and cabins, messdecks and galleys. On one famous occasion she was found in the Junior Ratings' Mess joining in a sing-song with the Yachtsmen and leading them in a rendition of *What Shall We Do With The Drunken Sailor*. However it wasn't long before she was discreetly but firmly led back to her own part of the ship. But Diana made her mark and a Royal Yacht Rating was heard to comment, 'There are 276 men on board *Britannia* and every one of them is in love with Princess Diana.'

Five years later *Britannia* hosted her final honeymoon for the Duke and Duchess of York who spent five days aboard the Yacht cruising the Azores. And so *Britannia* cast her magic over the four honeymoon couples, but not for long, for sadly each marriage was to fail.

Britannia, *the perfect romantic retreat*

Our aim was to give them a bit of peace and quiet, and I think we succeeded. Anywhere they wanted to go we took them. We wanted to make sure they had as happy a honeymoon as possible.

Rear Admiral Paul Greening

Britannia *graces the Solent during Cowes Week in 1996*

Sailing on a sunny day, with a fresh breeze blowing ... is the nearest thing to heaven anyone will ever get on this earth.

Princess Anne

The purpose-built inflatable raft was first used for transporting the royal Land Rover in 1956

Prince Andrew holds the anchor flag aloft at Fort William in 1967

Britannia *was a familiar sight at Cowes Week*

The Queen, Prince Andrew and Prince Edward wave as they leave Portsmouth at the start of the Western Isles Cruise in 1981

I was always struck by how much the Queen and her family enjoyed their holiday in Britannia *cruising the Western Isles. It seemed to be the Queen's only real holiday each year, away from official visitors.*

Captain David Hart-Dyke

High Days & Holidays

In 1864 when King Edward VII, then Prince of Wales, first competed in Cowes Sailing Regatta off the Isle of Wight, he gave the event the royal patronage that it has enjoyed ever since. Nearly a century later the Royal Yacht *Britannia* continued the tradition, when in 1955 she made the first of thirty-five proud appearances at Cowes, each time accompanied by the Duke of Edinburgh.

The Royal Family has grown up with a love of the sea, and for Prince Philip in particular the chance to take the helm of a Flying Fifteen or steer a single-masted Sloop was an annual highlight. As children, Prince Charles and Princess Anne learnt the ropes at an early age and during the 1960s would regularly crew for their father. But it was the sight of *Britannia* elegantly gracing the Solent, that made Cowes a special week for many people. After the week's event, *Britannia*, with the Queen on board, would set sail for Scottish waters. This was the start of the Queen's much cherished annual holiday to the Western Isles which would end with a stay at Balmoral.

Out of the public spotlight and surrounded by her family, the Queen had the chance to relax completely on the Western Isles Cruise. With only a small party of the royal household on board, this was as informal as life on *Britannia* ever got. During the cruise, the Queen would traditionally invite the Officers to dine with her and later the invitation would be returned when *Britannia's* Officers hosted a dinner party for the Queen and Prince Philip in the Wardroom. Sometimes the Yachtsmen would get together and put on an evening's entertainment for the Royal Family in the form of a carefully planned and well-rehearsed concert party.

While the Queen may have been at her most relaxed during the summer cruise, it was not so for the Officers for whom new challenges were added to their long lists of daily chores. Finding the perfect picnic spot - scenic, secluded, no midges - and forecasting the weather became daunting tasks. One Officer wryly remarked: 'The Western Isles cruise certainly tested the versatility and flexibility of all the Yacht's company.' To help them through the holiday, the Officers set down their collective knowledge in a booklet entitled *Western Isles Without Tears*. This little pamphlet contained many useful tips on how to avoid the pit-falls. Particular mention was made of barbecues. These were a royal favourite, and invariably came under the charge of Prince Philip: very bad news if someone forgot the matches or the wood brought from *Britannia* was fire-retardant, as happened on one infamous occasion. Fortunately the advice was generally heeded and these incidents were few and far between. On the whole Western Isles did pass without tears and provided some of the happiest and most relaxing times for the Queen and her family.

The Court Afloat

For a state visit some five tonnes of luggage, including everything from the Queen's jewels to the famous bottles of Malvern water for Her Majesty's tea, was brought on board and stowed in the ship's hold. With the Queen came forty-five members of the royal household, who along with Britannia's Officers and Yachtsmen, made sure that each visit ran like clockwork and that no detail was overlooked.

Most senior in the travelling royal household were the Queen's two Private Secretaries, Her Majesty's Press Secretary and the Master of the Household. Along with them came the dressers, valets, Buckingham Palace chefs, detectives, clerks, assistants, surgeon and hairdresser, not forgetting the ladies-in-waiting, equerries, pages, secretaries and footmen. Together they comprised a sort of floating court, each well versed in his or her duties, and all there to serve the Sovereign.

A daily routine was quickly established on board. The Private Secretaries worked with the Queen on Government business and made sure that official engagements went without a hitch. Each morning the Press Secretary would report on the previous day's media coverage, and the Master of the Household, who looked after domestic affairs on the Yacht, attended to everything from seating plans to the service of the food.

For a state visit, which would often be planned up to eighteen months in advance, the Foreign Secretary would embark with a team from Whitehall. During these occasions the cypher room on board the Yacht would be busy receiving and decoding Government messages as the whole business of state affairs carried on without interruption.

A member of the royal household carries Prince Charles' organic vegetables on board

During the state visit, every mind will be concentrated on whatever is required to provide the right setting for Her Majesty, but remaining inconspicuous will be a key task for most.

Commander Hugh Daglish

MEDICAL DEPARTMENT

Principal Medical Officer (PMO)

1 Chief Petty Officer (CPO) Medical Assistant
In charge of Sick Bay routine & assistant to PMO

1 CPO Medical Technician
Physiotherapist

ROYAL MARINES BAND

Director of Music

Colour Sergeant
The Drum Major

Colour Sergeant
The Bandmaster

5 Sergeant Bandsmen

8 Corporal Bandsmen

NAVIGATION DEPARTMENT

Commander N
Navigating Commander responsible for Navigation & Communications

Assistant Navigation & Meteorology Officer

Communications & Royal Cypher Officer

1 CPO Chief Radio Supervisor
In charge of Radio Sub-Department

1 CPO Chief Communications Yeoman
In charge of Tactical Signalling

2 PO Radio Supervisors

1 Petty Officer (PO) Communications Yeoman
In charge of Flag Deck & Message Distribution

SEAMAN DEPARTMENT

ADMIRAL

The Commander
Executive Officer & Second in Command

1 First Lieutenant
Fo'c'sle Officer

1 Second Lieutenant
Quarterdeck Officer

1 Chief Bo's'n's Mate
In charge of Seaman Department Activity

1 The Coxswain
In charge of Discipline & Administration

1 The Boatswain (Bo's'n)
In charge of Britannia's boats

1 The Royal Barge Officer
Also serves as Household Liaison Officer

The Queen's Coxswain
In charge of the Royal Barge

ENGINEERING DEPARTMENT

Commander E
The Engineer Commander & Wardroom Mess Secretary

Senior Engineer
Deputy to Commander E

1 Main Machinery Officer
In charge of main machinery

1 Outside Machinery Officer
In charge of auxiliary machinery, shipwrights & laundry

1 Electrical Officer
In charge of electrical services

Warrant Officer
In charge of logistics & personnel

3 CPO Marine Engineering Mechanics
In charge of Boiler Room

1 CPO Engineer Artificer
In charge of auxiliary machinery

2 CPO Engineer Shipwrights

2 CPO Engineer Artificers

1 CPO Electrician

SUPPLY DEPARTMENT

Commander S
The Supply Officer & Admiral's Secretary

The Keeper & Steward of the Royal Apartments

Deputy Supply Officer
Deputy to Commander S

Warrant Officer Writer
In charge of pay & the Admiral's office

1 CPO Steward
In charge of the Wardroom

1 CPO Caterer
In charge of catering & menu planning

2 CPO Stewards
Deputy & Assistant Keepers & Stewards of the Royal Apartments

1 CPO Cook
In charge of the Royal & Wardroom Galleys

1 CPO Cook
In charge of the Ship's Galley

Behind The Scenes

Who's Who In Britannia

Programming the activities of the Royal Yacht was a very complicated business. Careful coordination and thorough planning were fundamental to the smooth running of the Yacht. Like all Royal Navy ships *Britannia's* crew was organised into departments. The Admiral was in overall charge of his staff of twenty Officers and 240 Yachtsmen. He was supported by his Heads of Departments who organised work and delegated duties through the Sub-Departments.

6 Bandsmen   **4 Drummers**

2 Leading Radio Operators
Tactical Signalling Sub-Department

3 Leading Radio Operators
Radio Sub-Department

4 Radio Operators
Tactical Signalling Sub-Department

6 Radio Operators
Radio Sub-Department

1 Navigator's Yeoman

1 Waist Petty Officer
1 Fo'c'sle Petty Officer
1 Quarterdeck Petty Officer
1 Chief Quartermaster & Routines Petty Officer

Royal Marine Colour Sergeant
In charge of Royal Marines Detachment

Physical Training Instructor
Also in charge of between decks

3 Leading Seamen
1 Fo'c'sle Leading Seaman
1 Quarterdeck Leading Seaman

24 Able Seamen

4 Royal Marines
Part of Ship (Royal Deck), also Royal Marines Orderlies & Security Sentries

Commander's Office Writer
In charge of producing programmes, Daily Orders & Red Hot Notices

5 Petty Officer Marine Engineer Mechanics
With Part of Ship responsibilities

1 Petty Officer
In charge of the laundry

7 Leading Marine Engineer Mechanics
With Part of Ship responsibilities

24 Marine Engineer Mechanics
With Part of Ship responsibilities

8 Laundry Crew

2 PO Stewards
In the Wardroom

1 PO Naval Stores

1 PO Cook
Wardroom Galley

1 PO Cook
Ship's Galley

3 Wardroom Leading Stewards
1 Admiral's Leading Steward
3 Leading Stores Accountants
1 Leading Writer
4 Leading Stewards
1 Leading Airman
Photographer 'Snaps'

2 Wardroom Leading Cooks
2 Ship's Galley Leading Cooks

4 Wardroom Cooks
4 Ship's Galley Cooks

Royal Marine Butcher

8 Wardroom Stewards

2 Writers
Admiral's Office

8 Royal Stewards

Britannia *followed by a flotilla of admirers during the D-Day Review in 1994*

Signalling from the Flag Deck

Britannia's *Navigating Officers chart the ship's progress*

*The Admiral has said to me, in a most friendly way,
'If you get this wrong, nothing you've achieved since
joining will matter.' It was a statement of fact.*

Commander Hugh Daglish

A Tour of Duty

When a Yachtsman joined *Britannia's* crew he entered a world quite unlike any other in the Royal Navy. His orders were nothing less than to 'strive always for perfection'. The Yachtsmen's daily tasks involved a mixture of the awesome and the absurd. They ensured that the slope of the royal gangway was never steeper than 12°, and arranged the royal flowers. They dived daily to search the seabed beneath the Yacht, and polished every item of silver until it gleamed. In temperatures of up to 120°, they manned *Britannia's* 'state of the ark' laundry, yet had to appear as pristine as the ship herself at all times.

No woman ever served among *Britannia's* crew. Around half of the 240 Yachtsmen plus all of the twenty Officers were generally appointed to the Royal Yacht for a two-year tour of duty. The remaining hundred or so sailors were permanent crew and stayed with *Britannia* throughout their Naval career. For this they received no extra pay, allowances or leave. Promotion prospects were greatly reduced because advancement was only through 'dead men's shoes' when somebody left the Yacht's service. All were hand-picked to meet the very highest standards. And each and every one chose this special ship for the honour and privilege of personally serving Queen and Country.

The Queen chats to some of Britannia's *Royal Yachtsmen* during the South Pacific tour to commemorate her Silver Jubilee in 1977

As soon as the Queen comes out of her bedroom in the morning, I have to get in there quickly and get everything tidied up and make the bed before she comes back.

Mark Elliot, Leading Steward

Tropical Routine: Britannia's crew indulge in a spot of sunbathing during the Queen's 1961 cruise to Africa

Daily Orders

It was once observed that if the Navy were a monastic service, the Royal Yacht would be a silent order. No shouting, whistling or unnecessary noise of any kind was permitted. To preserve the tranquillity befitting a royal residence, orders were given by hand signal. The smooth running of the Yacht depended on the typed Daily Orders, which for a state visit would detail each day's programme down to the nearest half minute. If there were any last-minute changes, then the 'Red Hot' noticeboards came into operation. These boards, positioned throughout the Yacht, were used to post urgent orders and it was the duty of each Yachtsman to check them for instructions.

At the start of each tour, every Yachtsman was issued with a pair of starched white plimsolls. These kept noise to a minimum and helped to protect the two-inch-thick teak decks. The junior Yachtsmen had the arduous task of scrubbing the decks daily to keep them in pristine condition. So that the Royal Family were not disturbed, all work near the royal apartments had to be

carried out in silence and everything had to be completed by eight o'clock in the morning. If a Yachtsman did encounter any of the Royal Family, he was under strict instructions to stand stock still and look straight ahead until they had passed. It was also a Royal Yacht tradition that the sailors did not wear caps when near the royal quarters. Technically this meant that they were out of uniform and therefore saved the Royal Family from constantly returning their salutes.

Britannia was the only ship in the Royal Navy where Yachtsmen were called by their Christian names. In a tradition which went back to Queen Victoria's reign, even the Yachtsmen's uniforms differed from their Royal Navy counterparts. The junior ratings' distinctive black bow, worn on the back of their trousers, was originally introduced as a mark of respect for the Queen's late husband, Prince Albert. On *Britannia* too, the sailors wore their uniform tops inside their trousers, as opposed to outside like the rest of the Navy. And instead of the customary red

badges, Royal Yachtsmen wore blue badges.

Unlike all other Navy ships, *Britannia* had no punishment regime. Exemplary behaviour was expected at all times. There was no room for indiscretion or misdemeanour. If a sailor seriously misbehaved he would be dismissed immediately from the Royal Yacht Service. In 1981 the ship was rocked when a homosexual vice ring was uncovered on board which led to nine Yachtsmen serving jail sentences.

In this strict and confined environment, time out was essential. The sailors could retreat to the ship's funnel which housed a tiny multi-gym where they could do their physical exercise. Aerobics classes, led by one of the Petty Officers, were organised on the Foc's'le Deck. Wherever *Britannia* docked, games of football, cricket or rugby would be convened. For the less athletic, kite flying competitions, village fetes, hoopla and even Morris dancing all offered a chance to let off steam.

Everything on Britannia, *including the* Royal George *binnacle, was kept in pristine condition*

The sort of things we would go through in a three month deployment would be 2,200 toilet rolls, 250 gallons of Teepol [washing-up liquid], 244 tins of brasso, 250 pairs of gymshoes and 270 litres of white top coat paint.

PO Harry 'the B' Horne

A Royal Yachtsman scales Britannia's *mast*

Away for months at a time, Britannia's *Yachtsmen made their own entertainment horse racing on the Foc's'le Deck*

My abiding memory is not of places but of people, the Royal Yachtsmen, a ship's company who have no equal. I felt that I could call on them to do anything and it would be done, cheerfully, efficiently and quietly.

Lord Lewin

The Royal Barge was used to take the Queen and Prince Philip ashore

An Ambassador Abroad

The Royal Yacht *Britannia* has helped to make the Queen the most travelled monarch the world has ever known. From 1954 to 1997, *Britannia* carried the Queen and her family on 968 official visits, sailing some 1,087,623 nautical miles, the equivalent of once round the world each year. Wherever she went, from Bermuda to Bangkok, Rangoon to Reykjavik, the Royal Yacht was rapturously received by cheering ex-pats who lined the quaysides. For them, *Britannia* represented more than a ship: she was a little bit of Britain, a piece of the Commonwealth, the last vestige of the Empire. In the early years, the Queen had used the Royal Yacht as a very visible means of keeping in touch with the countries over which she ruled. Visits to Australia, Canada, Hong Kong and some of the remotest islands in the South Seas regularly featured in the Yacht's itinerary. Throughout her life the Royal Yacht called at over 600 ports in 135 countries, and on each and every occasion enabled the Queen to carry out her duties on her own terms and on her own ground.

Britannia sailed the seas for forty-four years, but while she remained constant, all around was changing. The once great British Empire was no longer a dominant power. Colonies were handed back and countries which had once come under British control gained independence. The political map of the world had altered and *Britannia's* role was shrinking. It was perhaps the Royal Yacht's final official duty which was the most symbolic and significant of her life. In June 1997 the Union Flag was lowered for the last time over Hong Kong, ending a century and a half of Colonial rule. As *Britannia* sailed out of Hong Kong harbour, carrying the ex-Governor General, now plain Mr Patten, back to the UK, the last chapter of the Empire closed.

The presence of the Royal Yacht was a brilliant stroke. To those who saw her, to say nothing of those who had the privilege of being invited on board, the experience was brilliant, symbolic and unforgettable.

Sir Patrick Mayhew

The Queen relaxes on the Royal Yacht, enjoying a dinner during her Silver Wedding anniversary cruise in 1972

Entertaining In Style

Britannia took Britain abroad, and she did it in inimitable style. When the Queen entertained on board it was, for the fortunate few who were invited, a chance to glimpse the 'unobtrusive excellence' of which *Britannia* was so justly proud.

An invitation to step on board the Royal Yacht and dine at the table of Her Majesty The Queen was the ultimate honour and the result of months, or sometimes years, of preparation. From the first approach by the host country to detailed discussions between the Foreign Office and Buckingham Palace, from reconnaissance visits by royal staff to the finalisation of an hour-by-hour itinerary, every event was orchestrated down to the last detail. Long before *Britannia* set sail guest lists were drawn up, invitations issued, menus printed, wines chosen and seating plans finalised.

The royal food was prepared by the Buckingham Palace chefs who were especially flown out to the ship when the Royal Family were embarked. With them would come one of the kitchen porters from the Palace. The Queen's chefs worked in *Britannia's* royal galley. Of the other two galleys on board, one was reserved for the Officers and the other for the ship's company. Before *Britannia* set sail, the holds, storerooms, refrigerators and coldrooms in the ship's lower decks were stocked high with meat, fish, vegetables, fresh, frozen and dried provisions. One hundred chickens could be roasted at a time in the ship's two Admiralty ovens, and the huge four-tiered steamer produced two hundred perfect puddings in a single batch. Two months' supply of meat and fish could be stored in *Britannia's* cold rooms, and the dairy and vegetable rooms held enough provisions to feed the whole ship for a month. Fresh bread was baked daily and where possible local

vegetables bought to supplement supplies. Wines were chosen in London and stored in the ship's wine cellar for use throughout the voyage.

For a state banquet dress was dictated by climate, but was always formal. For men black tie was *de rigueur*, while the ladies donned full-length evening dress. Tiaras were worn only by the Queen and female members of the Royal Family. Guests arriving at the Yacht would be welcomed on board by senior members of the royal household and invited to the Drawing Room for pre-dinner drinks. From there, the guests would proceed to the state Dining Room, each lady accompanied by a gentleman. While this was happening, the Queen, the Duke and their guests of honour posed for an official photograph before taking their places at the dining table. During the meal, often a five-course banquet, the ship's photographer, 'Snaps', would hastily develop the prints. Later the Queen and Prince Philip would find a discreet moment to leave their guests and sign the photographs, which would then be framed ready for presentation before the end of the evening.

After dinner, the Queen and her fifty-four guests took their place on the Verandah Deck to watch one of the evening's highlights: Beat Retreat.

This was performed on the quayside by the twenty-six members of the Royal Marines Band and normally lasted around thirty minutes. The band was embarked for all major tours and added much pomp to *Britannia's* presence. The Royal Marines' repertoire was vast and varied, and in addition to being able to play perfectly the national anthem of each country the ship visited, they could turn their hand to every type of music from classical to ceilidh. In keeping with royal protocol, they would wear any one of their twenty-six different uniforms as the occasion demanded.

With Beat Retreat over, the Queen and the Duke would bid farewell to their guests who were escorted to the royal gangway and saluted by the Yacht's senior Commander as they left the ship. By the time the Royal Family returned to the Drawing Room for a evening nightcap, frenzied activity by the fourteen Naval Stewards ensured that every item of furniture was back in its correct position and the room restored to its original order. While the Royal Family retired to bed, the sailors worked into the small hours of the morning washing every glass and plate by hand, polishing the silverware and tidying the apartments until not a single sign of the evening's party remained.

The men are ready to receive the Royal Party, the food is prepared, the state rooms and cabins at their gracious best. The Royal Yacht herself is gleaming from stem to stern. I examine every detail, the varnished woodwork, the burnished brass - not a thread out of place, not the faintest fingerprint to be seen.

Commander Hugh Daglish

A historic meeting with President Mandela in Cape Town in 1995

The Royal Marines Band perform Beat Retreat

The Commonwealth Heads of State gather on the Yacht's Verandah Deck in Cyprus, 1983

President and Mrs Yeltsin during the royal visit to Russia in 1994

The Queen presents President and Mrs Reagan with a signed photograph in 1983

Flying The Flag

Kings and Queens, Presidents and Prime Ministers made history standing on *Britannia's* decks. In the state apartments honours were awarded, men knighted, and business deals worth millions of pounds struck. Throughout each and every event, *Britannia* enabled the Queen to carry out her duties as Head of State, in superb style and in a truly unique manner.

As well as hosting royal banquets and receptions, holidays and honeymoons, *Britannia* was an ambassador for British business, promoting trade and industry around the globe. In 1968 *Britannia* embarked on the first of many commercial events which became known as Sea Days. These were organised by the British Government, sometimes in conjunction with blue chip companies, and were designed to promote Britain's export drive. An invitation to attend an event on *Britannia* was exclusive enough to

ensure the presence of key players, who might not have attended so readily, had the event been hosted in an hotel. For added kudos, on some occasions a member of the Royal Family would be present. In June 1992 Princess Anne attended a Sea Day, run by Scottish Financial Enterprise, when *Britannia* was berthed in the port of Leith.

The day's business, which saw millions of pounds' worth of deals transacted, was rounded off by an evening reception to which partners were invited. Estimates vary on the amount of business which *Britannia* secured for Britain. The Overseas Trade Board reckoned that £3 billion had been made for the Exchequer as a result of commercial days on *Britannia* between 1991 and 1995. Other sources consider that the Royal Yacht secured the same figure in exports during a single visit to India in 1993.

The Admiral welcomes Benazir Bhutto, Prime Minister of Pakistan, on board Britannia *in 1993*

Princess Alexandra presents an award during an investiture in Tokyo in 1997

Business leaders gather for a Sea Day in Dubai in 1997

Margaret Beckett, Minister for Trade and Industry, visits Britannia *in Japan in 1997*

Mrs Thatcher, with Rear-Admiral Sir Paul Greening, arriving on Britannia *in Melbourne in 1981*

Anyone who witnessed Britannia *bringing the Queen into Sydney, Cape Town or Boston; Rio de Janeiro or New York; the opening of the St Lawrence Seaway; Fleet Reviews or the D-Day celebrations will testify to the glamour and excitement that her immaculate presence invariably generated.*

HRH Prince Philip

The evacuees wade out to meet Britannia's boats

The Royal Chart Room was transformed into the Operations Centre

The evacuees filled every available space throughout the royal apartments

Glad to be in safe territory, the British evacuees arrive in London

The Evacuation of Aden

Kept away from the shore by the twelve mile limit rule, the British warships played an important role in maintaining contact with people on shore, but the special status of Britannia *allowed her to go in closer than military vessels and gave her a unique wartime evacuation experience which was said to have delighted the Queen.*

Navy News

In January 1986, *Britannia* had her most heroic moment. En route for Australia, where she was due to meet the Queen for a state visit to the Pacific Islands, the Yacht's Admiral received news that civil war had broken out in the former British colony of Aden, on the southern tip of the Arabian peninsula. Emergency calls were made to Whitehall and Buckingham Palace. The Queen sent orders that the whole ship, including the state apartments, was to be made available to the rescued evacuees.

Together with the Royal Navy's Indian Ocean patrol ships, HMS *Jupiter* and HMS *Newcastle*, the supply ship RFA *Brambleleaf* and the survey vessel HMS *Hydra*, *Britannia* played a prominent role in the rescue mission. The Royal Yacht's unique status allowed her to go closer to shore than the other vessels. *Britannia's* landing craft headed for the beaches and ferried some four hundred and thirty people back to safety. Mothers with babies and grandmothers were among those who waded out to reach *Britannia's* boats while shrapnel flew around the beaches engulfed by the fighting. On board the Yacht the Royal Marines Band serenaded the evacuees as they sailed from the burning city, in a gesture both eccentric and reassuring. Throughout the royal apartments, the evacuees, wrapped in towels and blankets, filled every available space as they bedded down in safety for the night. In all *Britannia* rescued 1068 people of fifty-five nationalities from war-torn Aden.

The Handover of Hong Kong

Queen Victoria ruled when Britain seized Hong Kong. One hundred and fifty-six years later it was her great-great-great grandson, Prince Charles, who presided as the colony was handed back to the people of Hong Kong. At the beginning of January 1997, *Britannia* set sail from Portsmouth on her last and longest voyage, calling at twenty-nine ports around the world. Some six months later, the Royal Yacht sailed up the Pearl River and into Hong Kong harbour to conduct her final royal duty and witness the historic handover of the colony.

British rule in Hong Kong ended on June 30th 1997 in an evening of spectacular ceremony. At the stroke of midnight, the Union Flag was lowered for the last time in the presence of the Prince of Wales, Governor Chris Patten and Prime Minister Tony Blair, marking the end not only of the colony but of British colonialism. The Royal Yacht sailed soon after midnight, her final royal duty complete; the epilogue of Empire over.

Hong Kong was Britannia's last berth in a foreign port

It has been the greatest honour and privilege of my life to share your home for five years and to have some responsibility for your future. Now Hong Kong people are to run Hong Kong. That is the promise and that is the unshakeable destiny.

Chris Patten, Governor General of Hong Kong

Prince Charles greets Prime Minister Tony Blair before the handover

Chris Patten leaves Hong Kong carrying the Union Flag

In a final symbolic gesture, the flag is lowered during the Farewell Ceremony

The Final Voyage

When *Britannia* sailed from Hong Kong back to Britain in the summer of 1997, her days were numbered. Three years previously the Government had announced that the Royal Yacht would be taken out of service. And so, on December 11th 1997 *Britannia* was decommissioned at Portsmouth Naval Base in the presence of the Queen, the Duke of Edinburgh and fourteen senior members of the Royal Family. Some 2,200 past and present Royal Yacht Officers and Yachtsmen, together with their families, came to witness the ceremony.

The decommissioning of *Britannia* was an event of great sadness for the Royal Family. Aboard *Britannia*, not only had the Queen and her family travelled the world, but the world - its statesmen and leaders - had come to them; their guests from Sydney to Samoa had been received and entertained as at a royal palace on British soil. To the Royal Family *Britannia* was more than a Ship

of State. Unlike the royal residences designed and built by past generations, *Britannia* was the supreme embodiment of the style and taste of the Queen herself. As the Royal Family witnessed the Paying-Off ceremony, tears were shed by the Queen. Such emotional attachment was inspired only in part by affectionate memories of happy times spent on board; the end of *Britannia* seemed to symbolise the end of an era.

As the Royal Family resigned itself to life without a Yacht, the fate of *Britannia* remained unresolved. Proposals were put forward by cities around the UK, all competing to secure the ship. In April 1998 the Government announced that *Britannia* was to be moored permanently at Edinburgh's port of Leith. Some six months later, in October 1998, the Royal Yacht welcomed her first visitors on board. The ship, which had once so closely guarded the Royal Family, was finally revealed to the public.

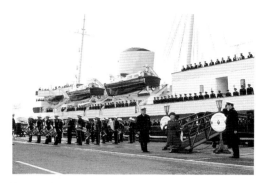

The end of an era as the Queen steps from Britannia *for the last time*

The decommissioning was an event of great sadness for the Royal Family

Britannia *approaches Edinburgh's historic port of Leith for her final berth*

Looking back over forty-four years we can all reflect with pride and gratitude upon this great ship which has served the country, the Royal Navy and my family with such distinction. My family and I extend our heartfelt thanks to all the Officers and Royal Yachtsmen for their unfailing loyalty, dedication and commitment to the Royal Yacht Service.

HM The Queen

Britannia Dossier

Laid down:
June 1952 at John Brown & Co. Ltd, Clydebank

Designer/Builder:
Sir Victor Shephard, Director of Naval Construction; and John Brown & Co. Ltd

Launched:
16th April 1953 by HM Queen Elizabeth II

Commissioned:
At sea, 11th January 1954

Length overall:
125.65m or 412ft 3in

Length on waterline:
115.82m or 380ft

Length between perpendiculars:
109.73m or 360ft

Maximum breadth moulded:
16.76m or 55ft

Breadths at upper deck moulded:
16.61m or 54ft 6in

Depth moulded to upper deck 45ft abaft midships:
9.90m or 32ft 6in

Depth moulded to upper deck at fore perpendicular:
12.29m or 40ft 4in

Depth moulded to upper deck at after perpendicular:
10.31m or 33ft 10in

Load displacement:
4,715 tons

Mean draft at load displacement:
5.2m or 15ft 7in

Gross tonnage:
5,862 tons

Shaft horsepower:
12,000

Speed:
22.5 knots maximum, 21 knots continuous

Engines:
Two geared steam turbines, developing a total of 12,000 shaft horse power. Two main boilers, and an auxiliary boiler for harbour requirements by Foster Wheeler

Range:
2,196 miles at 20 knots (burning diesel fuel)
2,553 miles at 18 knots (burning diesel fuel)

Main Mast Height:
42.44m or 139ft 3in - Royal Standard

Fore Mast Height:
40.54m or 133ft - Lord Admiral's Flag

Mizzen Mast:
36.22m or 118ft 10in - Union Flag

Fuel & Water:
330 tons of fuel oil providing a range of 2,000 miles at 20 knots
120 tons of fresh water. Additional tanks can increase fuel capacity to 490 tons and fresh water capacity to 195 tons

Propeller Diameter:
3.12m or 10ft 3ins

Pitch:
2.74m or 9ft

Developed blade area:
$5.17m^2$ or $55.7ft^2$

Tip clearance from hull:
0.84m or 2ft 9in

Maximum rudder torque:
125 tons ft at 14 knots astern and 30.5° angle

Rudder torque at 22 knots:
69 tons ft at 35° angle

Rudder torque at 15 knots:
33 tons ft at 35° angle

Maximum normal rudder force:
63.5 tons at 22 knots ahead, and 25.5 tons at 14 knots astern

Britannia's Deck Plans

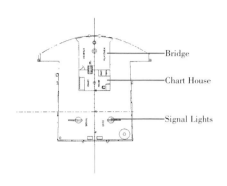

Bridge
Chart House
Signal Lights

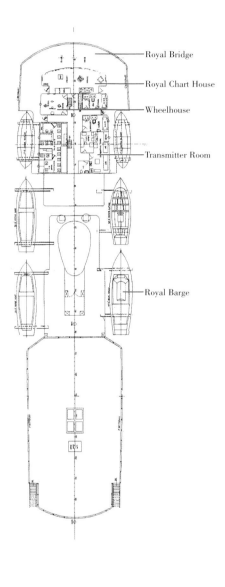

Royal Bridge
Royal Chart House
Wheelhouse
Transmitter Room
Royal Barge

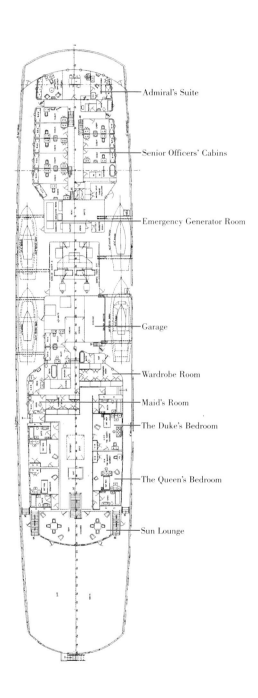

Admiral's Suite
Senior Officers' Cabins
Emergency Generator Room
Garage
Wardrobe Room
Maid's Room
The Duke's Bedroom
The Queen's Bedroom
Sun Lounge

Compass Deck   **Bridge Deck**   **Shelter Deck**

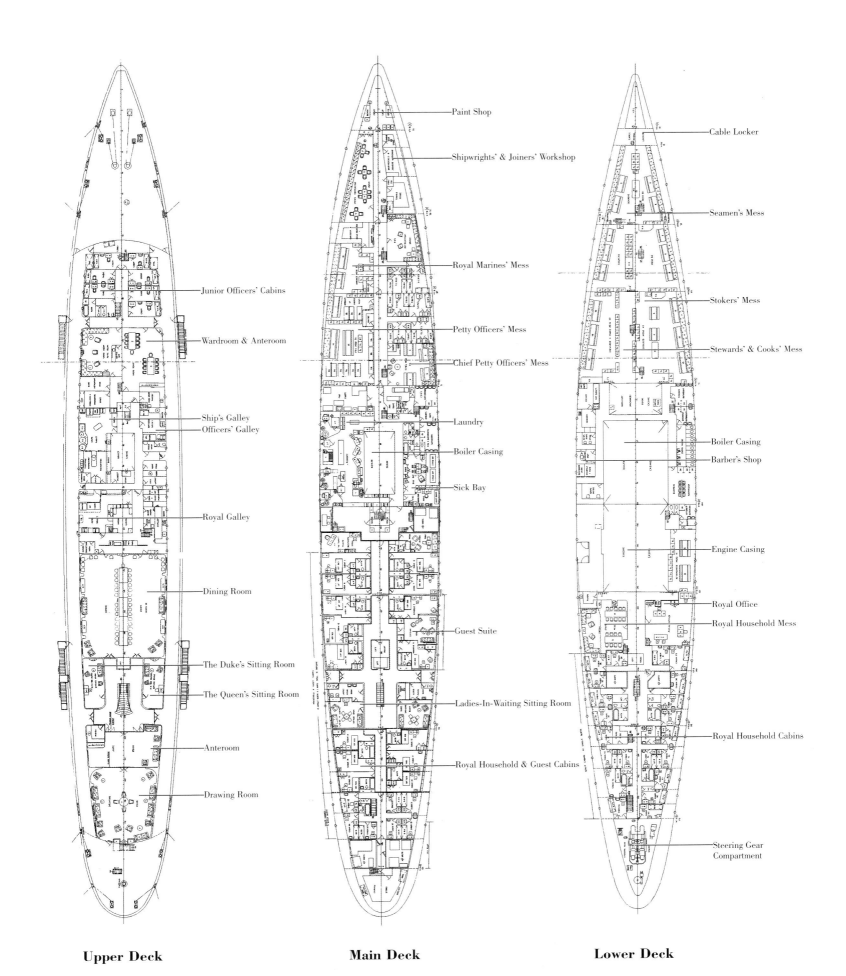

Upper Deck

Junior Officers' Cabins

Wardroom & Anteroom

Ship's Galley
Officers' Galley

Royal Galley

Dining Room

The Duke's Sitting Room

The Queen's Sitting Room

Anteroom

Drawing Room

Main Deck

Paint Shop

Shipwrights' & Joiners' Workshop

Royal Marines' Mess

Petty Officers' Mess

Chief Petty Officers' Mess

Laundry

Boiler Casing

Sick Bay

Guest Suite

Ladies-In-Waiting Sitting Room

Royal Household & Guest Cabins

Lower Deck

Cable Locker

Seamen's Mess

Stokers' Mess

Stewards' & Cooks' Mess

Boiler Casing

Barber's Shop

Engine Casing

Royal Office

Royal Household Mess

Royal Household Cabins

Steering Gear
Compartment

The Royal Family gather on the Verandah Deck during the last Western Isles cruise in 1997

Acknowldegements

Photography on board *Britannia* by Eric Thorburn, pages 6-27

Illustration page 18-19 by John Marshall

Illustration page 36-37 by Jim Proudfoot

All other imagery as follows:

© British Crown Copyright/MOD. Reproduced with permission of Her Majesty's Stationery Office: inside front cover, page 23 (bottom right), page 31 (top row, third row centre), page 32 (bottom left), page 33, page 39, page 41 (top left), page 42, page 46 (left & right), page 47, page 48 (second top), page 54

PA News: front cover, page 2, page 31 (2nd row left & bottom right), page 32 (top left, top right & bottom right), page 34 (top, bottom right), page 46 (centre middle), page 48 (bottom), page 49 (top & bottom right), page 50

Permission of the Trustees of The Imperial War Museum, London: page 23 (bottom left), page 31 (second row right, third row left & right), page 34 (bottom left, bottom centre & centre right), page 38, page 40, page 41 (right & bottom left), page 46 (top & centre bottom), page 48 (top & second bottom), page 49 (left & centre right), inside back cover

Partick Lichfield / Camera Press: page 28, page 44

Jayne Fincher: page 31 (bottom row left), page 32 (first column centre), page 35